CREATIVE EDUCATION • CREATIVE PAPERBACKS

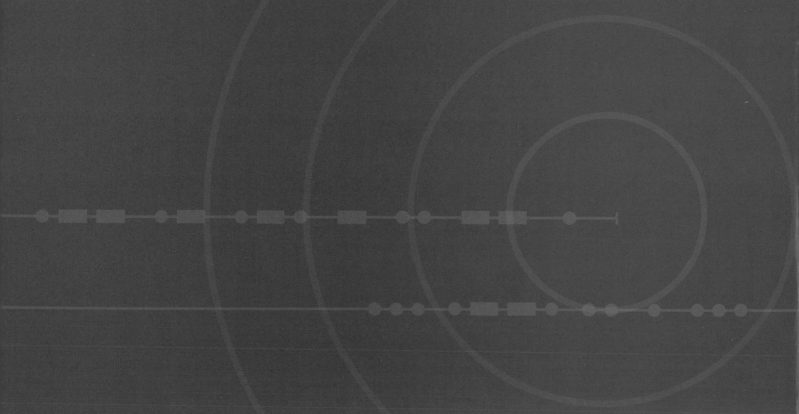

CIVIL WAR
SPIES

MICHAEL E. GOODMAN

Published by Creative Education and Creative Paperbacks
P.O. Box 227, Mankato, Minnesota 56002
Creative Education and Creative Paperbacks are imprints of
The Creative Company
www.thecreativecompany.us

Design and production by Chelsey Luther
Art direction by Rita Marshall
Printed in Malaysia

Photographs by Alamy (Everett Collection Inc, macdonald_stat-
ues, Mary Evans Picture Library, North Wind Picture Archives, The
Protected Art Archive), AP Images (Mike Groll), Corbis (Bettmann,
CORBIS, Medford Historical Society Collection, National Geograph-
ic Society), Getty Images (De Agostini Picture Library), Library of
Congress (Brady, Mathew B.; Brady's National Photographic Gal-
leries; Brady-Handy Photograph Collection; Civil War Photograph
Collection; Currier & Ives; Gardner, Alexander; Library of Congress),
Lost & Taken (Brant Wilson), Newscom (akg-images, Mathew Brady
Picture History), TextureX.com (TextureX), VectorTemplates.com

Library of Congress Cataloging-in-Publication Data
Goodman, Michael E.
Civil War spies / Michael E. Goodman.
p. cm. — (Wartime spies)
Summary: A historical account of espionage during the American
Civil War, including famous spies such as Elizabeth Van Lew, covert
missions, and technologies that influenced the course of the conflict.
Includes bibliographical references and index.
ISBN 978-1-60818-598-6 (hardcover)
ISBN 978-1-62832-203-3 (pbk)
1. United States—History—Civil War, 1861–1865—Secret service—
Juvenile literature. 2. Espionage—United States—History—19th
century—Juvenile literature. 3. Spies—United States—Biography—
Juvenile literature. 4. Spies—Confederate States of America—Biog-
raphy—Juvenile literature. I. Title.

E608.G66 2015
973.7'85—dc23   2014037530

CCSS: RI.5.1, 2, 3, 5, 6, 8; RH.6-8.3, 4, 5, 6, 7, 8, 9

First Edition HC 9 8 7 6 5 4 3 2 1
First Edition PBK 9 8 7 6 5 4 3 2 1

CONTENTS

SPYING FROM ON HIGH

On a sunny day in May 1862, Thaddeus Lowe looked down on the *Confederate* capital of Richmond, Virginia, seven miles (11.3 km) away, from a hot-air balloon he had built himself. The balloon known as *Intrepid* was attached to long ropes held by strong men on the ground to keep it from floating away. The *aeronaut* observed the fortifications built around Richmond and the movements of soldiers assigned to protect the city. He took notes and sketched a map. Suddenly, he saw a puff of white smoke and heard a loud bang. The Confederates were trying to shoot him down! If Lowe were captured, he might face hanging as a spy. He shouted to his ground crew, who frantically began to pull on the ropes, while Lowe released gas from the balloon. A second cannon blast sailed by the balloon as it descended and set down. It had been a narrow escape for a *Union* master spy.

THE NOT-SO-UNITED STATES

VISITORS TO THE UNITED STATES in 1860 would have noticed that the country was not as united as its name suggested. The northeastern and north-central parts of the country were mostly industrial with several large urban centers. The southeastern and south-central parts were mostly agricultural with more rural settlements than cities. To fill their agricultural needs, Southern plantations and farms required a lot of labor. The cheapest labor was provided by slaves. Southerners felt that slavery was essential for their region's economic survival. Slavery was also a large part of the area's history. The first Africans had been forcibly brought to Virginia

For hundreds of years, slaves picked cotton by hand on large farms in the American South.

in 1619. By 1860, slaves from Africa and elsewhere made up nearly 40 percent of the population in the Southern states.

Many Americans, particularly in the North, didn't look at slavery as an economic issue. They felt that it was morally wrong to control other people and treat them as property. They began demanding that slavery be ended in the U.S. at all costs—even if it meant going to war. Many Southerners felt that their way of life was being threatened. The turning point was the election of Abraham Lincoln as president in 1860. Lincoln was known to oppose any expansion of slavery into new states. Would he also strive to end the practice altogether? Southern leaders decided that they could not wait to find out. So, one month after the election, South Carolina voted to *secede* from the Union. Ten other states would soon follow, and together they organized a new country, the Confederate States of America (CSA), with former U.S. senator Jefferson Davis as its president.

To emphasize the separation, in the early morning hours of April 12, 1861, the Confederate army began shelling Union forces occupying Fort Sumter near Charleston, South Carolina. The first shots of the Civil War had been fired.

COVERT OPS
IRONCLAD INTELLIGENCE

Mary Touvestre was a slave in the home of the Confederate engineer tasked with rebuilding the CSS *Virginia*, an ironclad ship. One day in 1861, Touvestre heard the engineer brag that his iron-covered ship would soon help break the blockade the Union had on Confederate ports. She stole a set of his plans and walked all the way from Norfolk to Washington—around 140 miles (225 km)—to hand them over to the Union secretary of the navy. As a result, the Union navy sped up construction on its own ironclad, the *Monitor*. In March 1862, the *Monitor* engaged the *Virginia* in a historic battle that helped keep the blockade intact.

CHAPTER ONE

CIVILIAN *and* PROFESSIONAL SPIES

WHEN THE CIVIL WAR began in April 1861, neither the Union nor the Confederacy had a formal espionage network in place. Each side relied at first on military officers who volunteered to undertake dangerous missions while in disguise. These men knew that if they were caught, they risked lengthy imprisonments or executions. Being hanged was a common punishment for captured spies. One Union spy who could have won an award for most unusual disguise was Captain Peter Haggerty. He dressed up as an organ grinder (a street musician) and, accompanied by a pet monkey, walked through the streets of Baltimore, listening for pro-Southern *intelligence*.

Soon, the military officers were joined in spying by civilians who agreed to cross enemy lines. Most of the civilians chose to spy because they strongly supported the goals of either the North or the South. Many wore clever disguises and developed intricate *covers*. They pretended to be actors, doctors, peddlers, ministers, or even newsboys. The North often used slaves or former slaves as messengers. (There is no record of a slave ever spying for the Confederacy.) The South employed a group of doctors who transported documents hidden in their medical bags while making fictitious house calls.

From street performers (opposite) to battlefield ambulance workers (above), spies' covers varied.

Since most Americans looked alike no matter where they lived, it was not difficult for a spy to move between territories held by either side. It was also easy for a spy with acting ability to copy the regional accent that fit his or her cover. Spies in enemy territory did have to be cautious about little things, such as shoes and tobacco, though. Those two items differed from North to South. A Northern spy who wore the wrong boots or chewed the wrong brand of tobacco in a Southern city might find himself in trouble.

Some of the most successful civilian spies didn't even have to sneak behind enemy lines. They already lived in opposition territory and agreed to undertake secretive actions near their homes. The main difficulties they faced were fooling their neighbors and avoiding being detected and exposed. Two good examples of civilian spies were Elizabeth Van Lew, who organized an effective Union *spy ring* in Richmond, and Rose O'Neal Greenhow, who ran a Confederate espionage network in Washington, D.C.

Because they were women, Van Lew and Greenhow started their spy careers with a big advantage. In the 1860s, most men treated women politely, even those suspected of spying. Men also doubted that women could be devious enough to be spies or understand enough about military matters to be dangerous. So even when a suspected female spy was stopped, she was seldom searched or jailed. The first time Greenhow was arrested, she was allowed to change her clothes alone in her room. She swallowed a piece of paper containing a coded message and hid other incriminating information in her skirt. Even when she was imprisoned, she kept up her spying by wrapping coded messages around rubber balls and tossing them through the bars of her cell window to *agents* waiting outside.

Van Lew's gender aided her spying activities in Richmond, but her cleverness and attention to detail were just as important. She created her own personal code for messages and kept the key hidden inside a

SPY

*Widowed in 1854, Rose
Greenhow gradually
aligned herself with
Southern sympathizers.*

ring she never took off. She also helped avoid suspicion by sometimes dressing in ragged clothing and walking around the city mumbling to herself. Her neighbors began calling her "Crazy Bet" and would never have believed that the people the crazy lady met during her walks were fellow Union spies. Many members of Van Lew's espionage network were merchants and farmers living near Richmond. They did their spying while selling goods and produce to Confederate army units. Others were slaves and former slaves who worked inside Southern homes, including those of Confederate leaders. Black men and women blended in easily in the South, and because few of them were educated, white Southerners didn't think twice about talking strategy in front of them or leaving military papers and maps in plain view.

One slave-turned-spy was William Jackson, a coachman working for CSA president Jefferson Davis. Davis never even worried about discussing Southern military strategy with guests in his coach while Jackson was driving. Several times, Jackson risked his life by crossing the Union lines to report what he had learned about upcoming Confederate actions. One Northern general even wrote to Edwin Stanton, the Union secretary of war, praising "Jeff Davis's coachman" for providing key information before a battle.

As the war progressed, professional spy networks were established by both

President Lincoln met informants such as Pinkerton (left) in camps as battles moved from place to place.

sides. Two Northern *spymasters* were Allan Pinkerton and Lafayette Baker. Pinkerton had been a police detective in Chicago and then formed his own detective agency. During the early years of the war, Pinkerton was hired by a top Northern general, George B. McClellan, to gather intelligence about Confederate military movements and troop sizes. He was not very successful at these tasks. Pinkerton often exaggerated the number of Southern troops on the march. This caused McClellan to delay going into battle on several occasions for fear that his forces would be outnumbered.

Pinkerton was much more effective in the area of *counterespionage*. His

"CRAZY BET'S" CIPHER KEY

Elizabeth Van Lew created a special code for her messages. Only people who had the key could *decipher* the code. The key consisted of letters and numbers arranged in a 6-by-6 grid, with row and column numbers along the left and bottom. Van Lew's coded messages contained a string of numbers. Every pair of numbers stood for a letter. For example, if a number pair was 14, you would look for a place on the grid where row number 1 and column number 4 connected and find the letter "g." See if you can decipher this message: 13111133131153336143535 42625. Remember to start by breaking the numbers into pairs.

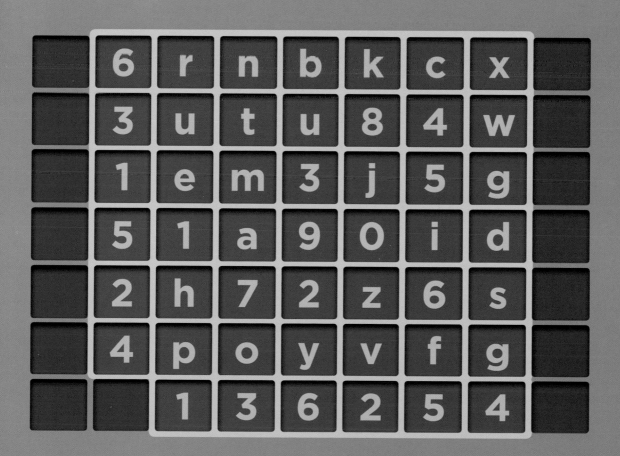

detective skills helped him uncover a number of Confederate plots. One of his big successes was arresting Rose Greenhow and putting an end to her Washington network.

Baker was also a counterespionage expert, but he and Pinkerton didn't work together. They were hired by different Union generals and conducted their investigations in very different ways. Baker was a violent man who often tortured suspects into confessions or revealing their associates' identities. However, he was not above taking bribes to let a suspect escape, and he got rich during the war. According to historian Nathan Miller, "No man in the history of American intelligence would have a more unsavory [nasty] reputation."

Southern military leaders also hired professional spies to go undercover and gather intelligence. One of the most unusual of these spies was Thomas Conrad, a Methodist preacher originally from Vermont but living in Washington in 1861. After the war broke out, the slavery-supporting Conrad moved south and was commissioned as a chaplain in the Confederate army. For his spy missions, Conrad often posed as a Union chaplain. In that role, he had no trouble penetrating Northern lines, where he could openly observe troops and talk about where they would be marching next. Later, he moved back to Washington and established a spy network there. Some of his best agents were *moles* in the Union War Department. These pro-Southerners had been employed at the War Department before the conflict began and simply stayed on the job, working for both sides at once.

Civilian and professional spies provided valuable intelligence, but newspaper reporters often supplied even more timely information. To feed the public's appetite for war news, major newspapers—particularly those in the North—had reporters on the scene before and after battles. If a Southern general wanted to know where Northern troops were heading, he could often discover the information in the morning papers. Robert E. Lee, the top Confederate general, was said to read five Union newspapers every morning with his breakfast to help plan his military strategy.

Union generals such as Ambrose Burnside found newspapers to be valuable resources as battles progressed.

CHAPTER TWO

TURNING *to* TECHNOLOGY

PEOPLE HAVE BEEN SPYING on each other in wartime for thousands of years. Up until the Civil War, most espionage activities fell under the category of HUMINT, which stands for human intelligence. Spies would use their own legs, eyes, ears, and hands to sneak around, observe, eavesdrop, and write messages—in plain language or codes. By the 1860s, new inventions such as the telegraph, hot-air balloon, and camera dramatically changed how spying could be done. The TECHINT (technical intelligence) era was beginning. TECHINT has become a dominant part of spying in the 20th and 21st centuries, but it was in its early stages during the Civil War.

No new invention altered Civil War spying more than the telegraph. When the war began, the telegraph had been in use for less than 20 years, but an extensive network of telegraph poles and wires already existed, particularly in the North. A Union spy who had gathered important intelligence no longer had to undertake a long and dangerous trip to deliver a report. Instead, by using a telegraph, he (or sometimes she) could get the information into the hands of military leaders as far away as Washington within minutes. Confederate spies also used the telegraph but not as effectively as Union agents. The South didn't

Recent technology such as cameras (opposite) and telegraph systems (above) relayed information.

The mixture of plaintext and symbols in a Confederate officer's diary signified use of a code.

have enough wire available to build its own wide-ranging network.

Spies on both sides also found that the telegraph could be a good way to "listen in" on enemy communications. How was that possible? In some cases, a telegraph operator could be persuaded or bribed to hand over copies of communications, or a mole could be placed inside the enemy's telegraph outpost to read and copy messages. One telegraph expert who worked for General Ulysses S. Grant, commander in chief of the Union army, even developed a way to "tap" the enemy's lines. He hooked a bypass wire onto a Confederate telegraph pole. The message still went through undisturbed, but Union telegraph operators could read it at the same time.

Southern telegraph experts soon began tapping Union lines, too.

When they realized this was happening, both sides started *encoding* many of their messages. Union agents managed to break most Confederate codes, but Confederate agents were not as successful. Still, there were enough un-encoded messages being sent that tapping could prove valuable. For example, a Southern telegraph expert named C. A. Gaston managed to tap a line connecting General Grant's Virginia headquarters with the White House in Washington. He was unable to decipher most of the coded messages but did intercept one un-encoded message telling where a large shipment of beef for Union soldiers was being delivered.

A Confederate general led his men on a raid the next day and captured the entire shipment.

The telegraph also provided a good means for tricking the enemy. Spies on both sides found ways to connect to the enemy's network and send out bogus messages. In spy talk, this is called *disinformation*. In 1863, a Confederate telegraph operator successfully confused Union military leaders with disinformation long enough to permit a Southern general to lead a damaging raid into Union-held Kentucky and march back into Tennessee without meeting any opposition.

While the telegraph allowed spies to send messages over land, the hot-air balloon made it possible for agents to "spy from the sky" for the first time in American warfare. Thaddeus Lowe, a 29-year-old scientist and aeronaut, approached Union generals with the idea of using hot-air balloons for espionage. In July 1861, he put on a demonstration in Washington for President Lincoln. Lowe ascended 500 feet (152 m) above the White House, while members of his team held onto the balloon with long ropes. Lowe had a telegraph key and transmitter with him, and telegraph wires were run

Finding where an army kept its main artillery (and how much of it was there) motivated spy work.

from the balloon to a receiver on the ground. From his perch in the sky, Lowe wired the president details about Confederate camps set up outside the capital and described troop movements he observed. Lincoln was impressed, and he appointed Lowe as the head of a new Union Army Balloon Corps.

As he observed the field of battle, Lowe transmitted telegraph messages to the War Department.

Over the next two years, Lowe and other members of his team spied on a number of battles in northern Virginia, and the information they provided was very helpful for Union commanders. They were particularly useful in helping gunners adjust their aim to successfully hit targets they couldn't see from the ground. The new invention worried Southern generals such as James Longstreet. "We felt secure until the Federals [Union army] began to realize all their advantages by floating balloons above our heads," he said. Several attempts were made to shoot down Lowe's balloons, but none succeeded.

Balloons had their problems, too. For one thing, they were sometimes hard to control, and balloonists worried about drifting and being forced to land in enemy territory. The balloons also often went into spins, causing their pilots to become too airsick to send reports. In addition, balloons were expensive to build and to operate. As a result, in 1863 Lowe requested a pay raise for himself and his balloon corps members from $6 to $10 a day. (The raise would have given each balloonist about the same pay as a Union colonel.) Lowe was accused of mismanaging what funds the Corps already had, and after his pay was docked, he resigned.

A third major technological development that influenced Civil War espionage was photography. The earliest known photograph was taken by a French inventor named Joseph Nicéphore Niépce in the mid-1820s, and the first photograph of a person was captured in late 1838 or early 1839. Then, in the 1860s, early photographers such as Alexander Gardner for the Union and A. D. Lytle for the Confederacy volunteered to use their cameras for spying.

NORTH OF THE BORDER

In April 1864, the Confederacy set up a secret office in Toronto, Canada. The office was supposed to send out agents to work undercover to encourage northwestern states (such as Indiana, Illinois, and Missouri) to threaten to secede if the Union didn't end the war and let the Confederacy stand. Another mission was to organize riots in several northern cities on Election Day in November 1864, in hopes of defeating Abraham Lincoln. The South spent a lot of money on its Canadian operation, but it ultimately failed—mainly because Union spies infiltrated the group and undermined its work.

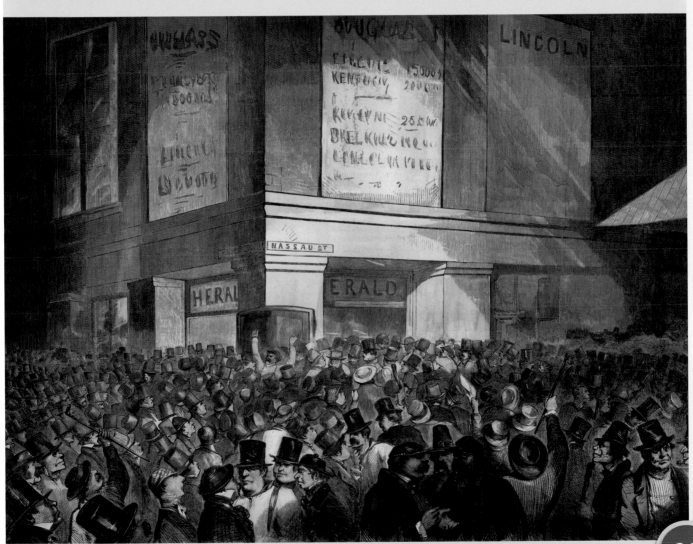

In the 1800s, the office buildings of major newspapers served as large-scale public posters.

While working with the Corps of Topographical Engineers (and later on his own), Gardner took photos for two spy-related purposes: (1) to help military engineers study the terrain and draw up maps needed to plan battle strategy; and (2) to capture group shots of Union units. Army commanders would then study these pictures to see if any of the soldiers looked unfamiliar and might be Confederates hiding undercover. Such methods were so effective that Confederate spies going undercover were warned never to appear in any photographs.

Lytle, who lived in Louisiana, was the best-known Confederate spy photographer. He had a special talent for slipping into Union camps and taking photos of troops, supply wagons, and artillery. When he had gotten all the information he could on film, he would go into his studio and develop the photos to share with Southern military commanders. To get soldiers in a Union camp to pose for him, Lytle would offer to provide free copies of any pictures he took of them. Everyone was glad to pose for photos and to answer questions about what they were doing. The troops were probably pretty upset when the promised pictures were never delivered!

Late in the war, Confederate photographers began using a new technique for developing photos small enough to be concealed inside the buttons of a messenger's coat and transported that way. Even if they were discovered, the images were almost too small to be recognized by the human eye. Military leaders needed to use a strong magnifying glass to discover what the pictures revealed. This was an early form of microfilm, a spy tool that would prove popular in later wars.

Gardner paid tribute to the Union scouts and guides as "men of iron nerve and indomitable perseverance."

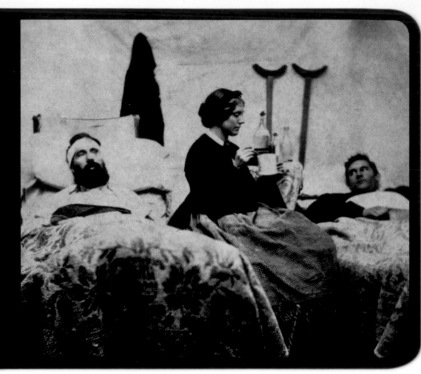

CHAPTER THREE

WOMEN GET *into* SPYING

BEFORE THE CIVIL WAR, most American women filled tradi-
tional female roles: they were wives, mothers, homemakers, and
sometimes teachers or nurses. What they were certainly not expected
to do was become soldiers or spies. Yet that is exactly what a number
of remarkable women did during the war.

You have already read in this book about two female spymasters—
Elizabeth Van Lew and Rose O'Neal Greenhow, who directed spy networks from their homes in enemy territory. Both women kept their
own agents busy and drove enemy counterespionage experts crazy.

Here are stories of just a few other women who carried out "unlady-
like activities" during the war:

Sarah Emma Edmonds served as both a soldier and a spy. She
changed her appearance and her role so many times during the war
that she probably could have been a successful actress. Edmonds was
born in Canada but ran away to the U.S. to escape her father's plans to
marry her off to an older farmer. She arrived in Michigan in 1860 with
a new identity—as a man named Frank Thompson. She was strongly
against slavery and looking for adventure.

When President Lincoln called for male volunteers to join the

Unlike other women who volunteered as nurses, Sarah Edmonds (above) participated in battle, too.

Union army, Sarah/Frank signed up. She was turned away at first because she was not tall enough but was finally accepted as a male nurse on the battlefields. Then she heard about an opening for a spy and volunteered. For her first undercover mission in Confederate-held Virginia, she decided to try an unusual disguise. She darkened her skin with dyes, put on a curly black wig, and assumed the role of a free black man. She managed to blend in and collected as much information as she could before crossing back over Union lines.

"Frank Thompson" went on several more missions, sometimes disguised as a white man and once as an Irish woman. She had a special gift for gaining strangers' trust and getting them to talk to her. These skills made her a valuable spy. She might have continued spying, but she became ill. She was afraid to go to an army hospital where her true gender might be discovered. So she checked into a civilian hospital and never returned to spying. Officially, she was listed as a deserter, someone who runs away from military duty. After the war, she became Sarah Edmonds again, married, had children, and wrote a popular book about her adventures. It took many years for Edmonds to clear her military record and be granted the army pension she felt she deserved.

Pauline Cushman worked as an actress before she became a Union spy. One night in Union-occupied Louisville, Kentucky, she shocked the audience by offering a toast in honor of Confederate president Jefferson Davis. Cushman was immediately fired from the play in which she was performing, but her pro-Southern cover launched her espionage career.

Over the next few years, Cushman undertook a series of missions for Northern commanders. The spying became more dangerous each time, and she had to make some daring escapes. Finally, near the end of the war, Cushman was stopped in Tennessee while carrying papers she had stolen from a Confederate army engineer. She was found guilty of spying and sentenced to death. Just days before the hanging, though, Union troops invaded the area where she was imprisoned and

Cushman's wartime exploits earned her acclaim and a final resting place in a national cemetery.

NEWSBOYS MAKE NEWS

Some of the youngest spies in the Civil War posed as newsboys for both sides. They could easily slip into an army camp with a stack of newspapers to sell. Once there, they would observe as much as they could and report their findings to their **handler**. In November 1864, a Union intelligence officer sent a report to General Ulysses S. Grant about a pair of newsboys who "have given [Confederate] General Lee much valuable information." He added that all he really knew about the boys was that "their names are Smith." General Grant also had his own newsboys/spies supplying him with useful intelligence.

In addition to the correspondents who traveled with the armies, newsboys were sent into the camps.

freed her. General James Garfield (a future U.S. president) awarded her the rank of brevet major in the army, and she was even commended by President Lincoln for her service. After the war, she developed a show in which she appeared onstage wearing a specially made Confederate officer's uniform and acted out some of her wartime adventures as a spy.

Mary Bowser gave up her freedom to become a spy. She and her parents were slaves for Elizabeth Van Lew's family. Van Lew freed all her family's slaves after her father died in 1843, but most, including Mary's parents, stayed to work as paid servants. Van Lew sent 10-year-old Mary to be educated in Philadelphia. The young woman returned home to Richmond in 1861 and married Wilson Bowser, another freed slave. She stayed close with Van Lew and agreed to take on a dangerous undercover mission for her friend. She joined the household staff of Jefferson Davis, posing as an illiterate servant. No one suspected that she could read or write, and no one knew that she had a photographic memory. She could recall perfectly almost everything she read or heard.

For two years, Bowser read military reports and overheard conversations and strategy sessions in the Confederate White House. She memorized information and shared it with other spies in Van Lew's network, who relayed it via coded messages to Union generals based in Virginia.

When stories of Bowser's activities leaked out after the war, Davis's wife Varina insisted that "an educated Negro woman" had never worked in her house. However, Bowser's espionage efforts were confirmed by other Richmond agents. Many years after Bowser died, a relative came across a diary with entries that mentioned a "Mr. Davis." She didn't understand the significance of the diary and threw it away.

The U.S. government appreciated Bowser's efforts, though. In 1995, she was inducted into the U.S. Army Military Intelligence Corps Hall

Davis's executive mansion in Richmond was built by banker John Brockenbrough in 1818.

of Fame. Her citation describes her as "one of the highest-placed and most productive espionage agents of the Civil War."

The Confederacy also had its undercover "heroes in skirts." One of the most famous was Isabella Marie "Belle" Boyd. She was born to a well-to-do family in what is now West Virginia. As a child, Belle was adventurous and loved to climb trees and race horses. Her family sent her to Baltimore to be educated, and then she briefly moved to Washington to become part of high society there. When the war broke out, she returned to Virginia and began spying on Union forces that occupied her hometown. The flirtatious 18-year-old coaxed secret information from Union officers and wrote down what she learned. She kept her notes inside a hollowed-out watch and had her slave deliver them to Confederate messengers.

Within a few months, Boyd was recruited as a courier (messenger) for several Southern generals. To pass through Union lines, she often posed as a young wife looking for her husband or a lost girl trying to get home. She was seldom stopped. When she was, she was usually let off with a warning.

That all changed a few months later when Boyd visited her aunt's house in Front Royal, Virginia. She learned about a plan to burn bridges around the town and trap Confederate general Thomas "Stonewall" Jackson's troops. She decided to warn the general herself. She disguised herself as a boy and made a fast, dangerous 15-mile (24.1 km) ride while dodging Union patrols. When Jackson got the message, he attacked quickly and won the Battle of Front Royal on May 23, 1862. Jackson awarded Boyd a medal for her service, but she also became a marked woman in the eyes of Union commanders. She was first arrested for espionage in July 1862 and imprisoned for a month but was set free. In 1864, she sailed to England, where she married a Union naval officer and became an actress. She returned to the U.S. in 1869 and in the 1880s became a popular speaker all around the country.

Jackson famously held his ground during the Battle of Bull Run (July 21, 1861), earning his nickname.

CHAPTER FOUR

SUPER-SPY HIGHS *and* LOWS

HUNDREDS OF MEN AND women spied for the North and South during the Civil War. Some of them stand out not only for the military successes their espionage enabled but also for the strange twists their spying careers took.

Timothy Webster was the Union's most successful **double agent**. Born in England, he immigrated to New York as a young man and joined the city's police force. Later, he was hired as a detective by Allan Pinkerton. Webster is credited with helping foil a plot to kidnap President Lincoln before his inauguration. When Pinkerton took over as a Union spymaster in 1861, he invited Webster to become one of his first **operatives**.

After carrying out several assignments in Tennessee and Kentucky, where he posed as a Northerner who supported the Confederacy, Webster undertook a series of missions to Richmond. On one trip, the boat he was on nearly sank during a storm. Webster survived and also saved several women and children. Suddenly, he was a hero in the South. The Confederacy's second secretary of war, Judah Benjamin, invited him to become a Confederate spy, and

Secret service agents hired by Pinkerton (opposite) were sometimes poached by Benjamin (above).

Webster quickly accepted. As a Southern "insider," Webster was even more valuable to the North. For example, he uncovered the identities of several Confederate agents working as moles in Washington, and Pinkerton rounded them up. Then Webster stopped filing reports for several weeks. Pinkerton worried about his "star" and sent two other agents to look for him. As it turned out, Webster had terrible *rheumatism* and couldn't get out of bed. Unfortunately, the men who went to find him were recognized as spies by Rose Greenhow, then living in Richmond. When they were arrested, the two gave up Webster in return for receiving lighter sentences. Webster was ordered to be hanged. Lincoln personally asked for mercy to be shown and even threatened that a Confederate spy would be hanged in retaliation, but the Confederate officials would not back down. Webster became the first Union spy to be executed on April 29, 1862.

Webster was not the only important Union double agent—and not the only one to fool Benjamin. New Yorker George Curtis also worked for both sides in the war. He started out as an infantry soldier, proving that he was brave and quick thinking. He kept calm, even when things seemed tense. Those traits brought him to Pinkerton's attention. Pinkerton hired Curtis as an operative and sent him to Richmond. There, he established a cover

as a salesman who could provide goods that were difficult for the South to obtain, such as gun caps and quinine, an important medicine. Curtis was introduced to Confederate general A. P. Hill, who gave him a pass to travel freely to and from Richmond and asked him to carry some reports to Benjamin. Curtis delivered the reports but not until after he had studied them. Benjamin was also impressed with the new "salesman" and entrusted some confidential messages to him, which Curtis copied before delivering. Curtis continued serving as a salesman and a courier throughout the war and was never unmasked as a

Virginian A. P. Hill resigned from the U.S. Army to join the Confederates as a colonel in 1861.

COVERT OPS
SAM STAYED SILENT

If you were to visit the Tennessee State Capitol in Nashville, you might be surprised to see a statue of a 19-year-old Confederate spy named Sam Davis. Davis was a member of a group of operatives known as Coleman's Scouts. He was captured in a Union raid in November 1863 and sentenced to hang. The Union commander offered to spare his life if he would reveal where the leader of Coleman's Scouts was. Amazingly, that man had also been captured and was standing only a few feet away. Davis refused to tell his captors anything, saying, "You may hang me a thousand times, and I would not betray my friends."

The grounds of Tennessee's capitol include statues of Davis (above), two presidents, and a World War I hero.

double agent. The fact that he always provided the goods he was paid to supply kept him from being suspected as a spy.

The South also had its super spies. Henry Harrison, a militiaman from Mississippi, became a top Confederate agent in Virginia soon after the war began. A trained actor, Harrison was a master of accents and disguises. In 1863, Harrison was assigned to work with Lieutenant General James Longstreet, whose troops were marching to join with Lee's forces in northern Virginia, preparing to invade Pennsylvania. Longstreet knew two important things about Harrison: (1) he had a reputation for providing thorough and accurate reports; and (2) he was being paid the outrageous sum of $150 a month for his spy work (worth around $3,000 today), so he must be good.

Longstreet gave Harrison a bag of gold coins and instructed him to "bring back information of importance." Harrison slipped through Union lines to reach Washington, where he met several Union officers for drinks. Their tongues loosened by alcohol, the soldiers told him that General George Meade was now in charge of Union forces and was marching his men into Pennsylvania. That meant that the Union troops were much closer to the Confederate army and posed more of a threat than Lee or Longstreet had thought. To counteract this threat, Lee decided to bring his troops together for a major offensive at the town of Gettysburg. The Confederate forces nearly defeated the Union army in the first day of fighting at Gettysburg but were eventually driven back after incurring heavy losses. Harrison's spy report had seemed helpful at first but proved damaging for the Confederacy in the long run.

For spies such as Harrison and Sarah Edmonds, the ability to change their appearance and speech patterns was key to their long-term success. By looking or sounding different on each mission, they kept spycatchers off guard. One Confederate agent nearly found himself in hot water because of such a disguise. The agent was

The bloody, three-day Battle of Gettysburg prevented further Confederate advances into the North.

After shooting the president, Booth broke his leg jumping down onto the stage and escaped the theater.

Thomas Conrad, the minister-turned-spy mentioned earlier. Conrad used different beard and clothing styles to slip past Northern counterespionage agents. On April 16, 1865, a week after the war ended, Conrad was still in Washington on a mission that had begun several weeks before. Unfortunately, the disguise he was using made him resemble John Wilkes Booth, the man who had shot President Lincoln two days earlier. Conrad was arrested by an overeager policeman and brought to the head of the Union Intelligence Service, Lafayette Baker, for interrogation. Although Baker had often tried to capture Conrad during the war, he now allowed the man to simply walk away, instead focusing his efforts on capturing the real Booth.

Another spy whose career took an unusual turn at the end was Antonia Ford. The daughter of a wealthy merchant and secessionist, Ford lived in

Virginia just outside Washington. For more than two years, Ford gathered intelligence from Union soldiers who were *quartered* in her family's large home and passed it along to Confederate officers. On several occasions, she drove her family's carriage across Union lines to deliver messages she felt she couldn't trust to anyone else. Then, in early 1863, a suspicious Union agent turned her in. Ford was imprisoned in Washington, but very little evidence could be found to prove she was a spy. That led her arresting officer, Major Joseph Willard, to begin working for her release. (Willard had also fallen in love with Ford while she was in prison.) Ford was released and in 1864 took an oath of loyalty to the Union. Ford and Willard then married. They had three children together, but their marriage didn't last very long. While in prison, Ford had contracted a disease that she couldn't shake. She died in 1871.

GENERAL STUART'S NEW AID.

"The rebel cavalry leader, STUART, has appointed to a position on his staff, with the rank of Major, a young lady residing at Fairfax Court House, who has been of great service to him in giving information," etc.—*Daily Paper.*

Ford was accused of passing information to General J. E. B. Stuart, under whom her brother served.

ONE COUNTRY AGAIN

FROM THE FIRING ON Fort Sumter to Lee's surrender at Appomattox, the Civil War was marked by four years of strife. Most of the battles were fought in the South, but young men from every state died in those skirmishes. Even more soldiers perished from the diseases contracted from unsanitary conditions in military camps or from terrible treatment they received as prisoners of war. In all, nearly 2.5 percent of the American population (as estimated in 1861) died in the war. The same percentage would amount to approximately 7 million American deaths today.

Passions were strong on both sides, and some of the most passionate men and women showed their support by spying to help their

Sitting at small tables in the parlor of the McLean House, Lee and Grant came to terms by exchanging letters.

side's army gain an advantage over its opponent. The spies used brain-power, deception, and new technological advances. They also pioneered methods that would become part of spycraft in future wars, particularly in the area of counterespionage. A large number of women took part in spying activities, possibly encouraging the postwar movement for women's rights and equality that gained steam throughout the country in the following decades.

Southerners had hoped to triumph in the Civil War by wearing down the Northerners and convincing them to give in to their demands to be allowed to form a new country where slavery could be maintained. Northerners had fought to keep the Union whole and to end slavery. By April 1865, the "reunited" country was still divided on the same issues. It would take many years to heal. But the "War Between the States" was over.

COVERT OPS
ROSE GREENHOW'S SAD END

After being banished to Richmond, Rose Greenhow traveled to Europe to raise support for the Confederacy. She charmed people in England and France and wrote a best-selling book. In August 1864, she sailed back home with a large amount of gold sewn into her dress. She planned to use the gold to help fund the war. Her ship struck some rocks off the coast of North Carolina, and Greenhow feared arrest. So she boarded a small boat and asked to be rowed to shore. A powerful wave struck the boat, throwing Greenhow overboard. The weight of the gold in her dress caused her to sink and drown.

CIVIL WAR
TIMELINE

NOVEMBER 6, 1860 — Abraham Lincoln wins the U.S. presidential election.

DECEMBER 20, 1860 — South Carolina secedes from the Union. Six more states follow by March 1861.

FEBRUARY 23, 1861 — Detective Allan Pinkerton sneaks Lincoln into Washington, evading a plot to kidnap the president-elect.

APRIL 12, 1861 — Confederate troops fire the first shots of the Civil War on Fort Sumter in South Carolina.

APRIL–MAY 1861 — Lincoln calls for volunteers to fight the Southern rebellion. Four more Southern states secede.

JULY 21, 1861 — Confederate forces turn back Union troops at the First Battle of Bull Run.

NOVEMBER 1861 — Julia Ward Howe, inspired after viewing General George B. McClellan's army near Washington, writes the lyrics to "The Battle Hymn of the Republic."

MARCH 9, 1862 — The ironclads USS *Monitor* and CSS *Virginia* battle to a draw at Hampton Roads, Virginia.

APRIL–JULY 1862 — The Union army marches on Richmond but is turned back in a series of battles by Confederate troops under Robert E. Lee.

SEPTEMBER 17, 1862 — The bloodiest single day of the war occurs at the Battle of Antietam in Maryland.

JANUARY 1, 1863 — Lincoln issues the Emancipation Proclamation, freeing slaves in the Southern states.

MAY 23, 1863	Union troops under Ulysses S. Grant begin the Siege of Vicksburg at the Confederate stronghold in Mississippi. The city falls on July 4, 1863.
JULY 1–3, 1863	Union forces soundly defeat Lee's army at Gettysburg, ending Confederate advancement into the North.
MARCH 9, 1864	Grant takes over as the commanding general of the Union army and begins a campaign in Virginia.
JUNE 9, 1864	Union forces begin the Siege of Petersburg near Richmond, putting Confederate troops on the defensive until the end of the war.
MAY–SEPTEMBER 1864	Sherman attacks and captures Atlanta.
NOVEMBER 8, 1864	Lincoln wins reelection.
JANUARY 31, 1865	Congress passes the Thirteenth Amendment, which abolishes slavery throughout the U.S.
APRIL 9, 1865	Lee surrenders to Grant at the Appomattox Court House in Virginia, effectively ending the war.
APRIL 14, 1865	Lincoln is shot at Ford's Theatre in Washington by John Wilkes Booth and dies the next day.

GLOSSARY

AERONAUT—the pilot of a balloon or airship

AGENTS—people who work for an intelligence service; spies

CONFEDERATE—a part of the league of 11 Southern states that seceded from the U.S. in 1860 and 1861

COUNTERESPIONAGE—efforts made to prevent or block spying by an enemy

COVERS—made-up occupations or purposes of agents

DECIPHER—to convert a coded message, or cipher, into normal text

DISINFORMATION—false or misleading intelligence, often provided by double agents or issued by an organization as propaganda

DOUBLE AGENT—a spy who pretends to work for one country or organization while acting on behalf of another

ENCODING—writing messages in secret code

HANDLER—a person who trains or is responsible for spies working in a certain place

INTELLIGENCE—information of political or military value uncovered and transmitted by a spy

MOLES—employees of one intelligence service who actually work for another service or who work undercover within the enemy group in order to gather intelligence

OPERATIVES—secret agents working for an intelligence group

QUARTERED—lodged or stationed in a home, sometimes through force

RHEUMATISM—a disease that causes pain and swelling in the joints

SECEDE—to withdraw formally from a group or organization, such as a union of states

SPY RING—a group of spies working together to carry out espionage

SPYMASTERS—people who recruit and are in charge of a group of spies

UNION—the league of mostly northern and western states that fought to keep the country together in the Civil War

SELECTED BIBLIOGRAPHY

Bakeless, John. *Spies of the Confederacy*. Philadelphia: J. B. Lippincott, 1970.

Caravantes, Peggy. *Petticoat Spies: Six Women Spies of the Civil War*. Greensboro, N.C.: Morgan Reynolds, 2002.

Hunter, Ryan Ann. *In Disguise! Undercover with Real Women Spies*. Hillsboro, Ore.: Beyond Words, 2013.

Jarrow, Gail. *Lincoln's Flying Spies: Thaddeus Lowe and the Civil War Balloon Corps*. Honesdale, Penn.: Calkins Creek, 2010.

Markle, Donald E. *Spies and Spymasters of the Civil War*. New York: Hippocrene Books, 1994.

Sakany, Lois. *Women Civil War Spies of the Union*. New York: Rosen, 2004.

Stevens, Bryna. *Frank Thompson: Her Civil War Story*. New York: Macmillan, 1992.

Sulick, Michael J. *Spying in America: Espionage from the Revolutionary War to the Dawn of the Cold War*. Washington, D.C.: Georgetown University Press, 2012.

WEBSITES

NATIONAL WOMEN'S HISTORY MUSEUM SPIES EXHIBITION
http://www.nwhm.org/online-exhibits/spies/2.htm
Brief biographies of notable women spies and descriptions of their espionage activities from the American Revolution to the Cold War.

SPYING IN THE CIVIL WAR
http://www.history.com/topics/civil-war-spies
A collection of articles, photographs, and videos provided by the History Channel. The site includes a small section on spying and extensive material on other aspects of the war.

NOTE: Every effort has been made to ensure that the websites listed above are suitable for children, that they have educational value, and that they contain no inappropriate material. However, because of the nature of the Internet, it is impossible to guarantee that these sites will remain active indefinitely or that their contents will not be altered.

INDEX